SPORTS SUPERSTARS

RADUCANU
RULES

SIMON MUGFORD   DAN GREEN

CONTENTS

HELLO EMMA!

Tennis ace **EMMA RADUCANU** is a

SPORTS SUPERSTAR

in the making. At just **18,** Emma won the **US Open** and has won millions of fans around the world with her powerful playing style and **positive, inspirational** approach to tennis.

THIS BOOK IS ALL ABOUT **HER!**

7

WHAT MAKES EMMA SUCH A **FANTASTIC** PLAYER?

TACTICS
She can vary her game to keep her opponent guessing.

RESILIENCE
Emma learns from setbacks and comes back stronger.

ATTACK TO WIN
Emma plays a strong, attacking style with lots of winning shots.

THE LINE QUEEN
Her fizzing power shots down the line help her win many points.

SUPER SERVES
Emma regularly delivers a first serve at more than 177 km/h (110 mph).

ONE OF A KIND

Emma began **2022** as the **NUMBER ONE** British female tennis player.

And ranked **13th** in the world.

Her **US OPEN** victory made her the **FIRST** British woman to win a major title since **Virginia Wade** in 1977.

Read about Virginia on page 107

She is the **ONLY** player to win a **Grand Slam** singles title as a **qualifier.**

Emma is the **ONLY** player to win a title after appearing in just **TWO** majors.

EMMA RADUCANU I.D.

NAME: Emma Raducanu

DATE OF BIRTH: 13 November 2002

PLACE OF BIRTH: Toronto, Canada

NATIONALITY: British

HEIGHT: 1.75 m

FAVOURITE SHOT: Forehand

BEST SURFACE: Hard

CHAPTER 2

LITTLE EMMA

Emma Raducanu was born in Toronto, Canada in **2002.**

Serena Williams was the US Open Women's Champion in 2002.

Emma lived with her dad **Ian** and her mum **Renee.**

The family left **Canada** and moved to **England** when Emma was two.

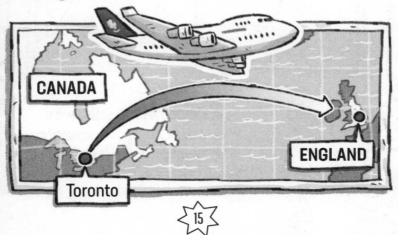

GLOBAL CITIZEN

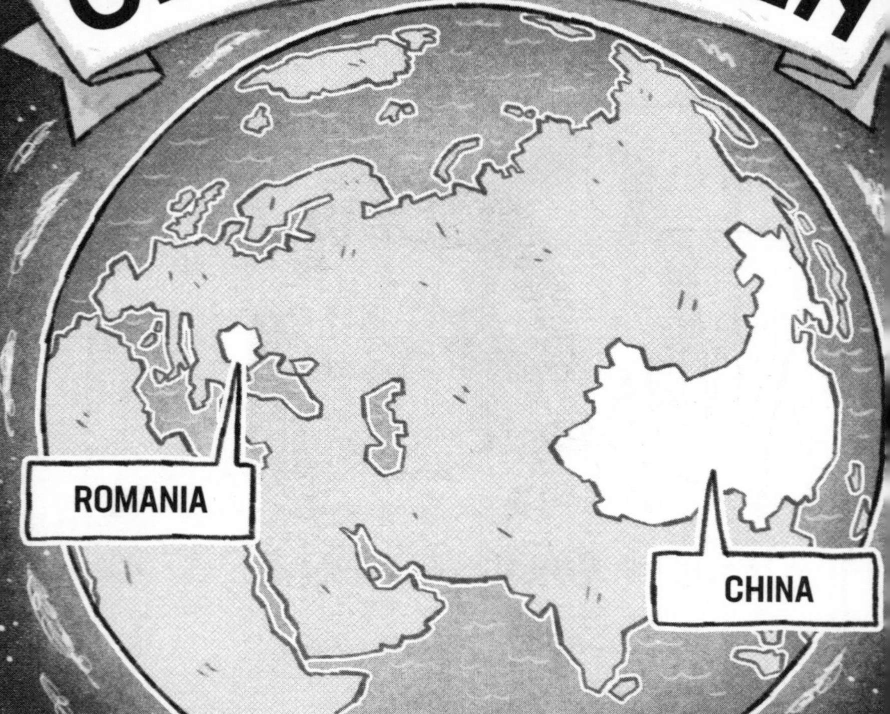

ROMANIA

CHINA

Emma's dad is from **Romania** in eastern Europe, and her mum is from **China.**

She is a citizen of both Britain and Canada and speaks **THREE** languages: **English, Romanian** and **Mandarin.**

In England, Emma lived with her family in the south London suburb of **Bromley.**

She went to the same secondary school as the super sprinter **Dina Asher-Smith.**

Fastest ever British woman

NEWSTEAD WOOD SCHOOL

SPORTS SUPERSTAR FACTORY

Emma's mum and dad encouraged her to take part in lots of **sports**.

She played **netball** . . .

. . . **football**

BOFF!

. . . basketball

. . . and even golf!

But from the age of five, there was one sport she was especially good at . . .

TENNIS!

But she didn't **ONLY** play tennis.

Emma's parents made sure that she did
some things that lots of
little girls like to
do, such as . . .

. . . **ballet**

Emma also did some things that **NOT MANY** little girls get to do. She was only **FIVE** when her dad took her to try go-kart racing.

EEEEOOOOW!!

F1 superstar *Lewis Hamilton* started out racing go-karts.

HAMILTON RULES

OUT NOW!

By the time she was **10,** Emma was leaping

over mud tracks on a **motocross bike!**

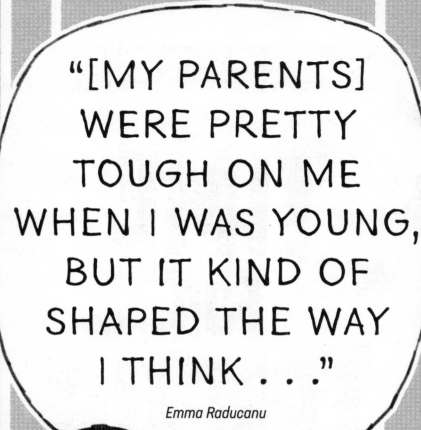

"[MY PARENTS] WERE PRETTY TOUGH ON ME WHEN I WAS YOUNG, BUT IT KIND OF SHAPED THE WAY I THINK . . ."

Emma Raducanu

CHAPTER 3

TIME
FOR
TENNIS

Back in medieval times, **'REAL TENNIS'** was played on a large, **indoor court** where the hard ball would bounce off the roof and walls.

It was played by rich lords and kings in France, Italy and England.

Henry VIII was a fan of the sport. He had his own court at **Hampton Court Palace.**

In the 19th century, outdoor games played on grass, such as **bowls, croquet** and **golf** became very popular.

The invention of the lawnmower helped!

WHIRR!

In the early 1870s, **Harry Gem** and **Augurio Perera** played a version of tennis on grass they called **PELOTA**.

They formed the very first **LAWN TENNIS** club in **Leamington Spa, England** in 1872.

At the same time as Harry and Augurio, **Major Walter Clopton Wingfield** had been playing his own version of tennis, which he called *sphairistikè*.

Major Wingfield created the **rules** and designed the **court** that is very much like the ones used today.

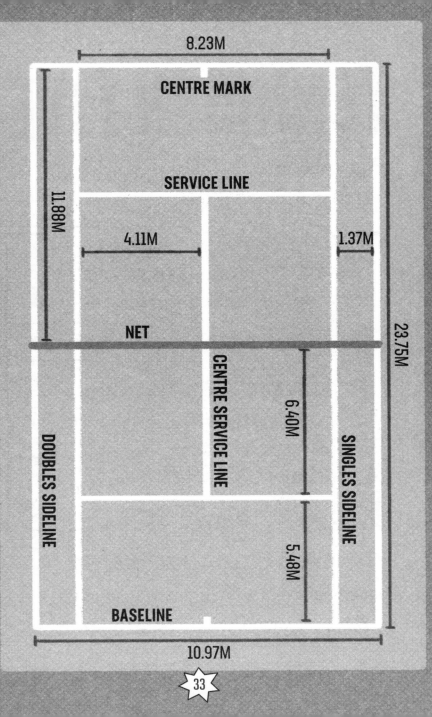

8.23M

CENTRE MARK

SERVICE LINE

11.88M

4.11M

1.37M

NET

23.75M

CENTRE SERVICE LINE

6.40M

DOUBLES SIDELINE

SINGLES SIDELINE

5.48M

BASELINE

10.97M

TENNIS IN FIVE

1 Tennis balls at Wimbledon were **white** until 1986.

Tennis strings were originally made from **sheep guts.**

3 In 2020, a world-record crowd of **51,954** watched Roger Federer and Rafael Nadal play a charity match.

In 2016 in Madrid, Spain, **1,474** people bounced tennis balls on rackets at the same – a world record!

5 Nobody really knows why zero points is called **'love'** in tennis.

In between the horse-riding, go-karting and motocross, Emma began to focus on tennis.

When she was **six,** Emma started training regularly at the **Park Langley Tennis Club** near her home.

Right away the coaches thought she was good enough to play in a **competition.**

YOU'RE A NATURAL, EMMA.

JUNIOR TENNIS

When you are little, a **full-size** tennis court is **huge!** So, kids aged 8 and under start by playing special versions of the game.

8 and UNDER

Court: 4.1 x 11.8 metres (quarter-sized)

Ball: Red (bigger and moves 75% slower than regular tennis balls)

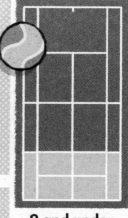

8 and under

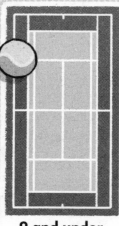

9 and under

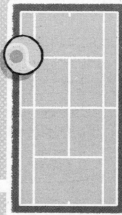

10 and under

9 and UNDER

Court: 6.15 x 17.8 metres
(three-quarter sized)

Ball: Orange (full-sized, but 50% slower than regular tennis balls)

10 and UNDER

Court: 8.2 x 23.7 metres (full-sized)

Ball: Green dot (full-sized, 25% slower than regular tennis balls)

11-year-olds play on *full-sized* courts with regular tennis balls.

TENNIS TITLES

When she was **six** Emma won a **Kent 8 and under** title - the first of many!

9 AND UNDER

Kent County Closed Junior Championships girls' singles

Beckenham LTA Winter Regional Tournament girls' singles

Bournemouth Open girls' singles

Graves Tennis Centre LTA Winter National girls' singles

10 AND UNDER / 11 AND UNDER

Cambridge LTA Winter National 10&U girls singles

Bressuire Tennis Europe 11&U girls singles

12 AND UNDER

National Tennis Centre LTA National Winter Tour Finals girls' singles

Braga Open, Portugal girls' singles

Bronze medal at the Winter European Cup with Great Britain

Fifth at the Orange Bowl girls' singles in Miami

14 AND UNDER

Bath Compete Open Tennis Festival (14&U and 16&U) girls singles

Zoetermeer Tennis Europe girls' singles

Road to Wimbledon finalist girls' singles

Roehampton Tennis Europe girls' singles

Nike Junior International Liverpool 18&U girls singles

Third at the Orange Bowl girls' singles in Miami

ITF JUNIORS

ITF Junior Tennis
Grade 4 Hamburg

ITF Junior Tennis
Grade 4 Oslo

ITF Junior Tennis
Grade 3 Chandigarh

ITF Junior Tennis
Grade 2 New Delhi

ITF Junior Tennis
Grade 2 Šiauliai Open

ITF Junior Tennis
Grade 2 Moldova

Junior Wimbledon
quarter-finalist

Junior US Open
quarter-finalist

JUNIOR HIGHLIGHTS

Youngest ever winner of the Nike Junior International 18&U (aged 13)

Junior Grand Slam Wimbledon debut aged 14

British Junior Number 1 aged 15

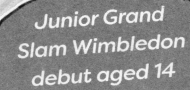

Beat Leylah Fernandez Wimbledon Girls 2nd Round 2018

CHAPTER 5

TENNIS TEENS

Emma's **US Open** win **aged 18** is a **FANTASTIC** achievement at such a young age.

She joins an **awesome** list of **tennis superstars** who picked up big wins in their teens.

Name: **Martina Hingis**

Country: **Switzerland**

Pro career: **1994-2017**

Grand Slam titles: **Five**

In 1997, Hingis won the **Australian Open** aged **16 years and 117 days** and became the youngest-ever world number 1 in the same year. She remains the **youngest female winner** of a Grand Slam title in the Open era.

Name: **Monica Seles**

Country: **Yugoslavia / USA**

Pro career: **1989-2008**

Grand Slam titles: **Nine**

The youngest-ever winner of the **French Open (16 years and 189 days** in 1990), Seles went on to win seven more Grand Slam titles before she was 20.

Name: *Tracey Austin*

Country: *USA*

Pro career: *1978-1994*

Grand Slam titles: *Two* 🏆🏆

Austin won the **1979 US Open** aged **16 years and 270 days,** and she is still the youngest ever winner of that title.

49

Name: Maria Sharapova

Country: Russia

Pro career: 2001-2020

Grand Slam titles: Five 🏆🏆🏆🏆🏆

Sharapova won **Wimbledon** - her first Grand Slam - in 2004, aged **17 years and 75 days.** She is the first Russian player to be ranked number 1 in the world.

Name: *Boris Becker*

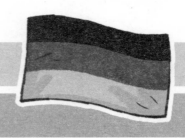

Country: *Germany*

Pro career: *1984-1999*

Grand Slam titles: *Six*

Boris 'Boom Boom' Becker is the youngest winner of the **Wimbledon** Men's title. He was just **17 years and 228 days** when he became champion in 1985.

Name: **Mats Wilander**

Country: **Sweden**

Pro career: **1981-1996**

Grand Slam titles: **Seven**

Wilander was unseeded when he won the **French Open** in 1982, aged **17 years and 293 days.** He remains (aged 19 years and 111 days) the youngest Australian champion in the open era.

Name: *Serena Williams*

Country: *USA*

Pro career: *1995-*

Grand Slam titles: 23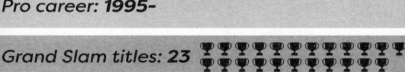

Active legend Serena won the US Open at **17 years and 357 days** - and then won **22 MORE Grand Slams**. Unbelievable!

POW!

Name: *Steffi Graf*

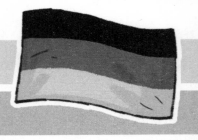

Country: *Germany*

Pro career: *1982-1999*

Grand Slam titles: *22* 🏆🏆🏆🏆🏆🏆🏆🏆🏆🏆🏆🏆🏆🏆🏆🏆🏆🏆🏆🏆🏆🏆

Graf took her first Slam - the 1987 French Open aged **17 years, 357 days.** She is the only winner (male or female) of each major at least four times.

Name: **Bjorn Borg**

Country: **Sweden**

Pro career: **1973-84, 1991-93**

Grand Slam titles: **11**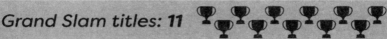

The Swedish sensation was **18 years and 10 days** old when he took the **French Open** in 1974. He is the first man to win five Wimbledon titles.

55

Name: **Rafael Nadal**

Country: **Spain**

Pro career: **2001-**

Grand Slam titles: **21**

Since winning the 2005 French Open aged **19 and 3 days,** Rafa has totalled 21 men's Slam victories.

CHAPTER 6

JUNIOR PRO

The **ITF Women's World Tennis Tour** is a series of tournaments for female tennis professionals.

They are held all over the world, with prizes from **$10,000** to **$100,000**.

Playing in these tournaments is the first step towards qualifying for the major competitions on the **WTA Tour,** such as **Wimbledon** and the **US Open.**

In **March 2018,** Emma was the **British Junior Number One.** She travelled with her dad to **Nanjing** in **China** to compete in two **$15K PRO TOURNAMENTS.**

In the first tournament, Emma went out in the qualifying third round. But the next time, she got all the way to the **quarter-final** of the main draw.

BRILLIANT!

It was a fantastic experience, and all the **hard work** and **training** was worth it.

FIRST PRO TITLE

DATE: **14–20 MAY 2018**

PLACE: **TIBERIAS, ISRAEL**

TOURNAMENT: **ITF $15K**

It was **blazing hot** under the desert sun, but Emma remained cool, easily beating her opponents to make it to the final.

WHACK!

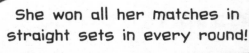

She won all her matches in straight sets in every round!

The final was tough, but she won in straight sets **7–5, 6–4,** lifting the trophy and collecting **$15,000** in prize money.

The win gave Emma her first WTA ranking – 885.

Her WTA ranking gave her the chance to qualify for **Wimbledon.** In the junior version, she played brilliantly.

The tennis world was beginning to take notice of Emma.

"FUTURE STAR!"

"HEAVY SERVE!"

EMMA'S 2018 PRO RESULTS

$15,000 NANJING, CHINA
QUARTER-FINAL

$15,000 TIBERIAS, ISRAEL

WINNER

$100,000 MANCHESTER, UK
1ST ROUND

WIMBLEDON, UK
1ST ROUND QUALIFYING

$25,000 LISBON, PORTUGAL
2ND ROUND QUALIFYING

$15,000 ANTALYA, TURKEY

WINNER

$25,000 WIRRAL, UK
SEMI-FINAL

CHAPTER 7

GRAND SLAM

SLAM TALK

The world's biggest tennis tournaments are the **Australian Open,** the **French Open, Wimbledon** and the **US Open.**

They are known as the **majors,** or the **GRAND SLAM** tournaments.

WINNING WORDS

Winning a **'GRAND SLAM'**, means winning all **four majors** in a **calendar year** (January to December).

Players who win all four titles, but not in the same year, win **a non-calendar year Grand Slam.**

A **career Grand Slam** is winning each of the tournaments over your career.

Why don't librarians like tennis?

There's too much **racket!**

ON THE SURFACE

Tennis is played mainly on three different surfaces: **hard, clay** and **grass.** The ball bounces differently and moves faster or slower depending on the surface.

The **US Open** and **Australian Open** are played on **hard courts**. They are slower than grass courts, but faster than clay.

MY BIG BOOK OF TENNIS COURTS
by ANNETTE

The **French Open** is played on **clay,** where the ball bounces high and moves slower.

Wimbledon has **grass courts.** The ball moves fastest on grass, and the bounce can vary.

MAJOR: AUSTRALIAN OPEN

FOUNDED: **1905**

VENUE: **MELBOURNE PARK** (SINCE 1988)

SURFACE: **HARD**

WINNER'S PRIZE (SINGLES): **AUS$2,875,000** (2022)

TOP WOMEN'S WINNER: **MARGARET COURT, AUSTRALIA** (11)

Known as the **Happy Slam** and held at the end of January, the Australian Open is the first Grand Slam event of the year.

MATCH POINT
The tournament was held in New Zealand in 1906 and 1912.

The Daphne Akhurst Memorial Cup

MAJOR: FRENCH OPEN

FOUNDED: *1891*

VENUE: *STADE ROLAND GARROS* (SINCE 1928)

SURFACE: *CLAY*

WINNER'S PRIZE (SINGLES): **€1,400,000** (2021)

TOP WOMEN'S WINNER: **CHRIS EVERT, USA** (7)

The French Open is held in May-June each year. Many players say it is the **hardest** of all the majors to play.

MATCH POINT
The trophy is made of pure silver.

The Suzanne Lenglen Cup

MAJOR: **WIMBLEDON**

FOUNDED: **1877**

VENUE: **ALL ENGLAND LAWN TENNIS AND CROQUET CLUB**

SURFACE: **GRASS**

WINNER'S PRIZE (SINGLES): **£1,700,000** (2021)

TOP WOMEN'S WINNER: **MARTINA NAVRATILOVA, USA** (9)

Wimbledon is the world's **oldest** tennis tournament. Most players think of Wimbledon as the **'one to win'**.

MATCH POINT
Players must follow a strict, all-white dress code.

The Venus Rosewater Dish

MAJOR: *US OPEN*

FOUNDED: *1881*

VENUE: *FLUSHING MEADOWS, NEW YORK*

SURFACE: *HARD*

WINNER'S PRIZE (SINGLES): *US$2,500,000* (2021)

TOP WOMEN'S WINNERS: *CHRIS EVERT, USA / SERENA WILLIAMS, USA* (6)

The US Open is the **last** Grand Slam tournament of the year and is held in **August–September** each year.

MATCH POINT
The trophy is made by Tiffany, the famous New York jeweller.

GRAND SLAM FIVE

Only **FIVE** players in history have won a singles Grand Slam.

DON BUDGE
(USA)
1938

MAUREEN CONNOLLY
(USA)
1953

ROD LAVER
(AUSTRALIA)
1962, 1969

MARGARET COURT
(AUSTRALIA)
1970

STEFFI GRAF
(GERMANY)
1988

CHAPTER 8

MOVING UP

In 2019, Emma continued to work hard - on **tennis** and at **school!**

BUZZ!

5:30 AM

SNOOZE

BUZZ

Emma **trained** every day before school. It was the year of her **GCSE exams** - and she **ACED** them - getting three 9s and four 8s.

WHOOP!

On the tennis court, Emma failed to qualify for Wimbledon, but won her **first ITF $25K title,** in Pune, India.

She finished the year ranked **374** in the world at the age of 17.

Emma was voted the *2019 LTA Girls' Player of the Year.*

Like everybody else, Emma's life changed in **2020** with the **Coronavirus pandemic.**

Tennis tournaments and training were cancelled. Emma **stayed home,** did her **school lessons online** and exercised.

$$f(x) = \frac{1}{2}(x^2 + 1), x \geq 0$$

Some tennis events began **without spectators** later in the year.

Emma played in a **mixed doubles** match against **Andy Murray** - and **WON!**

WELL PLAYED GUYS.

Emma ended 2020 as the **LTA Girls' Player of the Year** - again - and winner of the **British Tour Masters** title.

CRACK!

Then it was back to studying and training.

Emma had her **A Level exams** coming up, as she prepared for what was to become the **biggest year** of her tennis career so far!

WHOMP!

In 2020, tennis fans on social media tipped Emma for a bright future:

"Emma is a star in the making."

"She's seriously good!"

"A rising star!"

"There is no limit to what she can achieve."

"Future British Number One!"

CHAPTER 9

THE WILD CARD

108 players qualify for the Wimbledon Ladies' Singles based on their world ranking. **12 places** are available to players who come through a qualifying round.

The tournament organisers then choose **EIGHT** more players – **WILD CARD** entries.

Emma was handed a Wimbledon wild card in **2021.**

ANDY MURRAY and SERENA WILLIAMS also had Wimbledon wild cards in 2021.

ANDY MURRAY

SERENA WILLIAMS

GORAN IVANIŠEVIĆ

GORAN IVANIŠEVIĆ is the only player to win the Wimbledon men's singles title as a wild card. He did it in 2001.

YAY!

Emma faced Russian player **Vitalia Diatchenko** in the first round. The first set was very tight, but Emma won **7–6.** She won the next set without losing a game.

BLAM!

GO EMMA!

She followed that with wins over **Markéta Vondroušová** and **Sorana Cîrstea**. Emma was through to the **fourth round.**

Emma is the *youngest* British woman to reach the Wimbledon fourth round in the Open Era.

5 JULY 2021

COURT NUMBER ONE, WIMBLEDON

EMMA RADUCANU (GBR) **VS AJLA TOMLJANOVIĆ** (AUS)

On the day known as **_Manic Monday,_** when every men's and women's fourth round match is played at Wimbledon, Emma went on court at 8pm.

Emma's opponent was **ranked 75th,** but Emma matched her in the early stages. Tomljanović **won the first set.**

The **crowd cheered** Emma on, but she had difficulty concentrating and playing well.

Emma had to **retire** from the match as she had trouble breathing. Her dream debut at Wimbledon was over.

91

Playing tennis at the highest level is **EXTREMELY** physically and mentally **demanding.**

Emma had got very far, very quickly. Some commentators questioned if she was **tough enough,** but lots of others gave their **support.**

"THE COUNTRY IS PROUD OF YOU . . . ONWARDS AND UPWARDS."

Marcus Rashford

EMMA HAD JUST GOT STARTED.

Emma won **£181,000** at Wimbledon and her rank rose to **175.**

WIMBLEDON IN FIVE

1 The longest match at Wimbledon lasted **11 hours and five minutes.** It was between John Isner and Nicolas Mahut in 2010.

2 More than **54,000 balls** are used at a Wimbledon Championship. They are stored in giant fridges.

3 The fastest Wimbledon serve was hit by Nick Kyrgios in 2019. It was recorded at **230.1 km/**

4 **24 tons of strawberries** are eaten by spectators at Wimbledon each year.

5 **Rufus the Hawk** flies above the courts to scare pigeons away!

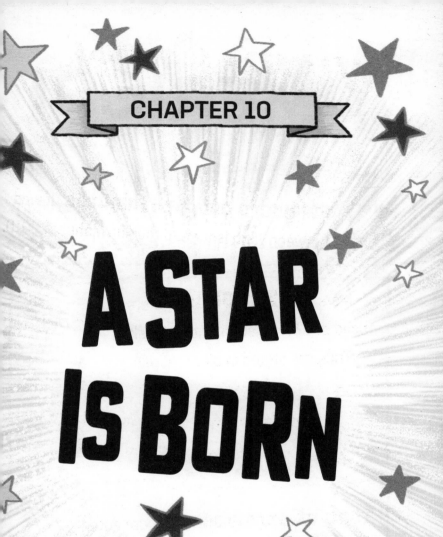

CHAPTER 10

A STAR IS BORN

AMERICA!

After Wimbledon - and having received brilliant **A Level results** - Emma travelled to the **USA.**

Emma's parents stayed at home because of **Coronavirus restrictions.**

She reached the final of a tournament in Chicago, then prepared for the **US Open qualifiers.**

Emma swept through the qualifiers in **straight sets!** She was going to play her **second Grand Slam** tournament.

THE ROAD TO THE FINAL

Emma beat . . .

Stefanie Vögele,

Zhang Shuai,

Sara Tormo,

Shelby Rogers,

Belinda Bencic,

and Maria Sakkari . . .

GRRR!

. . . to reach the **FINAL** of the **US OPEN!**

It was an incredible achievement.

And she did it in
straight sets!

She shot up the world rankings - and
became the **British Number One.**

AMAZING!

Emma's opponent was another teenage star – the 19-year-old Canadian, **Leylah Fernandez.**

British tennis legends **Virginia Wade** and **Tim Henman** were in the crowd. Millions of people around the world watched on TV.

The two young women were evenly matched, but it was Emma who had the edge. She recovered from a cut to her leg to fire home an **ACE** at match point and win **6–4, 6–3.**

BOOM!

UNBELIEVABLE!

Emma's Wimbledon exit was all but forgotten. She played with **confidence** and **style** to win. The Bromley schoolgirl was a

GLOBAL TENNIS SENSATION.

Emma won an amazing **$2.5 MILLION** in prize money!

THE FAIRYTALE OF NEW YORK

EMMA WAS THE:

First British woman to win a **Grand Slam** singles title since Virginia Wade won Wimbledon in **1977**.

First qualifier to **win** a major in the Open Era.

Youngest British player to win a **Grand Slam title**.

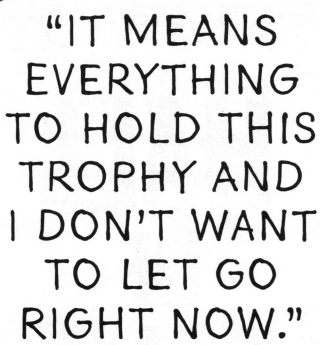

"IT MEANS EVERYTHING TO HOLD THIS TROPHY AND I DON'T WANT TO LET GO RIGHT NOW."

Emma Raducanu

104

Could **Emma Raducanu** join the
TENNIS HALL OF FAME?

Billie Jean King

A pioneer in women's tennis and equality in sport, Billie Jean King won 12 Grand Slam titles, six of those at Wimbledon.

Virginia Wade

The last British woman to win a major singles title before Emma, Wade won Wimbledon, the Australian Open and the US Open.

Margaret Court

Between 1960 and 1973, Court won 24 Grand Slam singles titles, more than any other player in history.

John McEnroe

Famous in the 1970s
and 80s for his on-court
outbursts and battles with
Björn Borg, McEnroe won
Wimbledon three times and
the US Open four times.

THIS IS HOW YOU DRAW
ME? **YOU CANNOT
BE SERIOUS!**

Andre Agassi

One of only eight male
winners of a career Grand
Slam, Agassi also added an
Olympic Gold to become one
of only two men to hold a
career Golden Slam.

Steffi Graf

Graf dominated the women's game in the late 1980s and 1990s. In 1988, she became the first player to win all the majors and the Olympic Games gold medal in the same year, known as the Golden Slam.

POW!

Agassi and *Graf* got married in 2001.

Martina Navratilova

Navratilova made the Wimbledon final 12 times (nine in a row) and won it nine times, the most for a female player.

Björn Borg

The 'ice-man' won the French Open six times and Wimbledon five times. He did much to make tennis the popular sport it is today.

Ivan Lendl

Lendl won eight Grand Slam titles from 1984 to 1990. He popularised the modern style of powerful baseline tennis.

Serena Williams

Williams has won 23 Grand Slam singles titles – the most in the Open Era. Along with her sister Venus, Serena brought a powerful, athletic style to women's tennis.

Roger Federer

Considered by many as the greatest player of the modern era, Federer holds the record for Wimbledon titles (eight).

Rafael Nadal

Famous for his great rivalry with Federer, the Spanish Nadal has won an incredible 21 men's Grand Slam singles titles.

Novak Djokovic

Djokovic has won 20 Grand Slam singles titles, including a record nine in the Australian Open and has been World Number One for a record total of 360 weeks.

Andy Murray

The most successful British player in the modern game, Murray ended a 77-year wait for men's Wimbledon champion when he won the Championships in 2013.

The world reacted with joy and offered its **congratulations** after Emma's incredible win in New York . . .

"IT IS A REMARKABLE ACHIEVEMENT AT SUCH A YOUNG AGE, AND IS TESTAMENT TO YOUR HARD WORK AND DEDICATION."

Her Majesty The Queen

"ABSOLUTELY UNBELIEVABLE . . . AN INSPIRATION TO EVERYONE."

Jack Grealish

"A STAR IS BORN – EMMA RADUCANU MAKES HISTORY . . ."
Martina Navratilova

"EXTRAORDINARY!"
Simona Halep

"CONGRATULATIONS CHAMP!"
Ant and Dec

"MADE UP FOR YA SISTER . . . YOU SMASHED IT."
Liam Gallagher

Liam looking thrilled

After the **Coronavirus pandemic,** Emma's story of **hard work, self–belief** – and a **spectacular win** – gave the world something to smile about.

She was suddenly very, **VERY** famous.

On **TV** . . .

On giant **billboards** . . .

and mixing with the biggest celebrities at the **Met Gala** in **New York.**

Then it was time to go back home to Bromley - and to see her **mum** and **dad.**

At the end of 2021, Emma was named

BBC Sports Personality of the Year

in recognition of her
fantastic achievement.

EMMA RADUCANU 2021

She also received an **MBE** in the Queen's
New Year Honours.

Britain's brightest tennis star
has a **fantastic future** ahead.

RADUCANU RULES!

QUIZ TIME!

HOW MUCH DO YOU KNOW ABOUT EMMA RADUCANU? Try this quiz to find out, then test your friends

1. Where was Emma born?

---

2. Which athletics star went to the same school as Emma?

---

3. Which motorsports did Emma try when she was little?

---

4. How old was Emma when she became the British junior number one?

---

5. In which country did Emma win her first pro tournament?

---

6. What is the name of the venue where the US Open is held?

----

7. Who was Emma's opponent when she retired at Wimbledon?

----

8. What injury did Emma suffer in the US Open final?

----

9. Who was the last British woman to win a major before Emma?

----

10. Who was Emma's opponent in the US Open final?

The answers are on the next page *but no peeking!*

ANSWERS

1. Toronto, Canada

2. Dina Asher-Smith

3. Go-karting and motocross

4. 15

5. Israel

6. Flushing Meadows

7. Ajla Tomljanović

8. A cut to her leg

9. Virginia Wade

10. Leylah Fernandez

TENNIS WORDS YOU SHOULD KNOW

Ace
A serve that is not touched by the receiving player to win a point.

Court
The rectangular area marked with lines on which matches are played.

ITF
International Tennis Federation

LTA
Lawn Tennis Association

Ranking
Players are given a standing according to their success in various tournaments.

Set
A sequence of games in match. Sets are usually won by winning at least six games and two more games than the opponent.

Serve
The tennis shot that starts the point.

HAVE YOU READ ANY OF THESE OTHER BOOKS FROM THE *SUPERSTARS SERIES?*

SPORTS SUPERSTARS

MORE COMING SOON!

FOOTBALL SUPERSTARS

5 FOOTBALL SUPERSTARS
STERLING
RULES
- FACTS
- STORIES
- STATS
SIMON MUGFORD ★ DAN GREEN

6 FOOTBALL SUPERSTARS
HAZARD
RULES
- FACTS
- STORIES
- STATS
SIMON MUGFORD ★ DAN GREEN

7 FOOTBALL SUPERSTARS
RASHFORD
RULES
- FACTS
- STORIES
- STATS
SIMON MUGFORD ★ DAN GREEN

8 FOOTBALL SUPERSTARS
VAN DIJK
RULES
- FACTS
- STORIES
- STATS
SIMON MUGFORD ★ DAN GREEN
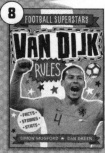

9 FOOTBALL SUPERSTARS
SALAH
RULES
- FACTS
- STORIES
- STATS
SIMON MUGFORD ★ DAN GREEN

10 FOOTBALL SUPERSTARS
NEYMAR
RULES
- FACTS
- STORIES
- STATS
SIMON MUGFORD ★ DAN GREEN

11 FOOTBALL SUPERSTARS
AGÜERO
RULES
- FACTS
- STORIES
- STATS
SIMON MUGFORD ★ DAN GREEN

12 FOOTBALL SUPERSTARS
POGBA
RULES
- FACTS
- STORIES
- STATS
SIMON MUGFORD ★ DAN GREEN

3 FOOTBALL SUPERSTARS
DE BRUYNE
RULES
- FACTS
- STORIES
- STATS
SIMON MUGFORD ★ DAN GREEN

14 FOOTBALL SUPERSTARS
MANÉ
RULES
SIMON MUGFORD ★ DAN GREEN

15 FOOTBALL SUPERSTARS
SOUTHGATE
RULES
- FACTS
- STORIES
- STATS
SIMON MUGFORD ★ DAN GREEN

16 FOOTBALL SUPERSTARS
ZLATAN
RULES
- FACTS
- STORIES
- STATS
SIMON MUGFORD ★ DAN GREEN

7 FOOTBALL SUPERSTARS
HAALAND
RULES
- FACTS
- STORIES
- STATS
SIMON MUGFORD ★ DAN GREEN

18 FOOTBALL SUPERSTARS
MARTENS
RULES
- FACTS
- STORIES
- STATS
SIMON MUGFORD ★ DAN GREEN

19 FOOTBALL SUPERSTARS
BRONZE
RULES
- FACTS
- STORIES
- STATS
SIMON MUGFORD ★ DAN GREEN

COLLECT THEM ALL!

ABOUT THE AUTHORS

Simon's first job was at the Science Museum, making paper aeroplanes and blowing bubbles big enough for your dad to stand in. Since then he's written lots of books about everything from dinosaurs and rockets, to BMX bikes, football and motorsport. He lives in Kent with his wife and daughter, a dog, two tortoises and a cat.

Dan has drawn silly pictures since he could hold a crayon. Then he grew up and started making books about stuff like people's jobs, football, big machines, space, *Doctor Who* and *Star Wars*. He lives in Suffolk with his wife, son, daughter and a dog that takes him for very long walks.